£5.50

conte

nts

Words: Eddie Rowley and
Kathryn Rogers
Design: Louise Ivimy

Published by
Grandreams Limited, Jadwin House
205-211 Kentish Town Road,
London NW5 2JU

Printed in Belgium

ON THE COU

CH...RONAN

What's your worst feature? My teeth.

What's your best feature? My eyes.

Do you have an inny or an outy belly button? An inny.

Are you a happy person? I try to be.

What was your most embarrassing moment? Forgetting lyrics on stage.

Do you believe in ghosts? I keep an open mind because if I don't, they'll come and haunt me. So, maybe, I do believe in ghosts.

Do you believe in UFOs? Kind of. Yeah, I do believe in them.

Where did you learn about sex? At school. We had sex education classes and all the guys used to fall around the place laughing. You know what guys are like!

Do you ever get lonely? I think most people experience loneliness. I certainly do and I go looking for affection, whether it's from my mother or from a relationship.

Do you get angry? I do. But I seldom explode. I normally manage to keep it in, which is not necessarily a good thing.

What do you wear in bed? Boxer shorts.

How old were you when you had your first proper date? I was 16 and it was a bit of an ordeal because I was very shy.

What's your biggest fear? Snakes.

How do you like to be considered? As a good, true friend.

When did you last cry? It was a long time ago and I was missing somebody.

What's your most frightening dream? I have a recurring dream where I'm running up stairs and my feet get caught. I can't move or run and there's somebody after me. I wake up with my heart pounding.

Is there anyone else you would like to be? No. I'm happy the way I am.

Do you consider yourself to be handsome? No. Far from it. I don't know what the fans see in me. I can't see it when I look in the mirror.

Did you ever work before joining Boyzone? I worked in a shoe shop when I was at school and for a while before Boyzone started up.

What would you have done if you hadn't joined Boyzone? Probably acting, but more likely I'd be working in New York, just like my brother and sister.

What's your bedroom like? It's an absolute mess. There are clothes everywhere. I haven't seen me carpet for six months.

Have you got a hidden skill? No.

Are you a tough guy? Well, I don't consider myself to be a tough guy. But if I had to defend myself I wouldn't back away.

What has been your happiest moment? Being in Boyzone.

What was your saddest moment? I've never had one. The day Boyzone finishes will be my saddest moment.

Do you fear the future? No. I look forward to the future.

girl

WHAT DO YOU LIKE MOST ABOUT GIRLS?

RONAN:
I like girls to be themselves.

KEITH:
The fact that they are feminine. I like girls to be feminine.

SHANE:
I just love women in general.

STEVE:
Their personalities, as long as they are natural and not putting on a show.

MIKEY:
Their bodies.

WHO IS YOUR FAVOURITE ACTRESS?

RONAN:
Meg Ryan.

KEITH:
Julia Roberts.

SHANE:
I don't have one.

STEVE:
Michelle Pfeiffer.

MIKEY:
Michelle Pfeiffer.

WHAT WOULD TURN YOU OFF A GIRL?

RONAN:
Someone who pretends she's something she's not.

KEITH:
If she was really masculine.

SHANE:
Smoking.

STEVE:
If she was false.

MIKEY:
A bad personality.

zone

WHO IS YOUR FAVOURITE SUPERMODEL?

RONAN:
I don't have one.

KEITH:
Eva Hertzigova.

SHANE:
I don't like models.

STEVE:
I don't have one.

MIKEY:
Claudia Schiffer.

WHO WAS YOUR DREAM WOMAN AS A TEENAGER?

RONAN:
I didn't have one.

KEITH:
Beth from Neighbours. I always had a soft spot for her.

SHANE:
Melanie Griffith.

STEVE:
Julia Roberts.

MIKEY:
Michelle Pfeiffer.

WHO IS YOUR FAVOURITE FEMALE SINGER?

RONAN:
I like lots of female singers, but I don't have a favourite.

KEITH:
Louise.

SHANE:
Madonna.

STEVE:
Janet Jackson.

MIKEY:
Alanis Morissette.

ON THE COU

CH...KEITH

Are you a happy person? Yeah, I'm a happy-go-lucky type of bloke.

Were you a model student at school? I was a bit of a bully, but not too bad. I was once suspended for letting off stink bombs.

Did you do well at school? Yeah. I got a good Leaving Certificate (A Levels).

Were you popular when you were a teenager? The girls seemed to like me. That made me unpopular with a lot of guys.

How old were you when you had your first kiss? I was 11 and in fifth class at primary school. She was a gorgeous little thing.

Do you remember the first girl you went out with? Yes, it was Shane Lynch's sister, Alison! I was 15 and we went out together for three weeks.

Were you ever dropped by a girl? Yes. When I was 16 I went out with a girl who was 21, but she didn't want to know me after our first date.

Do you remember the girl who gave you your best ever snog? Yes. It was my girlfriend Lisa Smith.

What's your worst feature? Probably my broken teeth.

What's your best feature? Probably my broken teeth as well, judging by the comments from some of the fans.

What was your most embarrassing moment? One time I went down to my local shopping centre and there was a door with no glass in it, so I stepped through it. When I returned later I tried to do the same again, but they had put the glass in and I bashed into it. Lots of fans saw the incident!

Do you believe in ghosts? I believe in spirits.

Did you ever have a near death experience? Yes. I was with Shane from Boyzone when he crashed his car two years ago. I injured my back and couldn't train.

Would you ever be tempted by any of your fans? No. I wouldn't mess around with them.

What was your most unusual job? I worked at a golf driving range, picking up all the balls.

How did you learn about sex? There was a course in school.

What's your biggest fear? That my career will end suddenly without me wanting it to.

When did you last cry? When my baby was born because it was a very emotional time in me life.

What is your most frightening dream? I was going over a cliff in a car, but I woke up before I hit the bottom. Itwas very frightening. My heart was pounding when I woke up.

Is there anyone you would like to be? I'm pretty happy with who I am.

Have you got a hidden skill? I had a bit of a flair for architectural drawing.

What was your happiest moment? Meeting me girlfriend and having the baby.

What was your saddest moment? I haven't had one.

Do you fear the future? No. I look forward to it.

	Who would you like to be stranded on a desert island with?	Who would you not like to be stranded on a desert island with?
Ronan	I don't really rely on other people.	Chris Evans.
Keith	My girlfriend Lisa.	Chris Evans because I'd kill him.
Mikey	Claudia Schiffer.	Eamon Dunphy (Irish journalist).
Shane	My car.	Simply Red.
Steve	Mr Bean, to make me laugh.	A politician.

Stra

What three personal items would you take with you?	What personal comfort would you miss?	What song would you sing to help you cope?
Toothbrush, clean underwear and some music.	A nice soft bed.	Any song.
Me car. Me jewellery. Me baseball cap.	Me double bed.	'Always Look On The Bright Side Of Life'.
Guitar, suntan lotion and a cold bottle of milk.	My Levi jeans.	Any song by John Lee Hooker.
Toothbrush, spot cream and tweezers.	Me Ma.	'I'm Coming Home Now'.
A walkman, a book and me mam.	A soft bed.	All the Boyzone songs.

nded

Stargazing...

Mikey's date of birth: 15/08/72

Star sign: Leo

Element: Fire

• • • • • • • • • • • •

Key characteristics: Confident, dominant, warm, loving, dynamic

Key faults: Proud, arrogant, condescending, selfish, conceited

WHAT THE STARS SAY ABOUT MIKEY

Leo in profile

King of the jungle and of the zodiac, Leo the lion has a regal air about him. Mikey, as a Leo, is proud and courageous and has a sense of dignity that marks him apart from other signs. Leos are warm, generous, open and affectionate.

Leos are also dynamic, fiery individuals that like being the focus of attention. They are at their best in the glare of the spotlight. They can't stand being overshadowed.

Mikey should take care that he doesn't take himself too seriously at times as Leos can become conceited. Leos feelings of self-importance can bring out the bossy, domineering and arrogant side of Leo nature.

Leo in work

Leos naturally rise to the top of the pile in the workplace. They are born leaders and have an ability to command respect. They love being the centre of attention and they love applause. Leos have got all the skills needed to get to the top of any field they choose.

Leo in love

People are naturally drawn to extrovert Leos. Warm and loving, it's unusual to find a Leo without a partner as they love to love and be loved. They are loyal, faithful, fun partners. They are warm, generous and protective. They like to be the centre of attention, but once they get plenty of cossetting, they're not so much lions but pussycats!

Zodiac girls for Mikey

Leos will get on best with fellow fire signs, Sagittarius and Aries. Air signs Gemini, Aquarius, and especially Libra, also make good partners for Leo.

Water signs, Pisces, Cancer and Scorpio are too 'wet' for fiery Leo and plodding Earth signs, Taurus, Virgo and Capricorn, can smother Leo's enthusiasm and zest for life.

Other famous Leos

Neil Armstrong

Fidel Castro

Queen Elizabeth

Terry Wogan

Danny La Rue

Mikey and the stars

Do you read your horoscope everyday?

No. I think the whole idea of horoscopes is stupid.

Does this profile of Leo resemble you in anyway?

I suppose it does in some ways. I like taking the lead and I enjoy being the centre of attention when I'm on stage, but I like my privacy also and I like to get away from the spotlight quite often. I don't think I could be described as arrogant or condescending either. At least I hope not!

You don't believe in star signs or horoscopes?

No. When you think about it, how could the position of planets on the day you were born affect your personality and your entire life? It doesn't make any sense.

mum

Mother knows best, so we talked to Boyzone's mums to discover the real Boyz. The mums certainly revealed all! Read on to discover some of the embarrassing childhood secrets of Boyzone!

SHANE'S MUM, NOLEEN LYNCH

Why did you call him Shane?
I was going out with his dad, Brendan, since I was 13 and one of the first pictures we went to see was a cowboy film called Shane. We always said if we ever had a boy we'd call him Shane. As it happens he's the only boy, he's got five sisters.

What day was he born on?
Saturday.

What sort of a child was he?
Quiet, Shane was always a quiet child. Until the fashion show this year, that is!
(Shane dropped his trousers at the huge Supermodel Fashion Show in Dublin earlier this year.)

What was his favourite toy as a child?
Cars. It was always cars. He had hundreds of them.

Did he like school?
He always hated school from junior class upwards, but he was never any trouble. There was never any hassle at school or anywhere else. He was a very quiet child.

Can you remember any funny incident with Shane as a child?
He demented us to go to Disneyland when he was very young. All he talked about was seeing Mickey Mouse, so, when he was about three, we went to America for three weeks.
On the second day we went to Disneyland. We only arrived and he met Mickey. He shook his hand and had a photo taken with him and then he turned around and said, "OK, can we go home now?" That was it, he had lost interest and just wanted to go straight home to his cars after that.

zone

As a child, what did he want to be when he grew up?
He wanted to be a truck driver and drive all over the world. It was always cars and trucks and in the end he went to work with his dad in the garage. We always assumed that's where he would go and he was in his 2nd year apprenticeship as a mechanic when he left to go with Boyzone. Even if he's not driving them, he ends up sitting in the back of trucks and vans all day now anyway, so I suppose he got what he was looking for in one way!

What were his hobbies?
BMX racing, running and swimming, but never football.

Did you ever think he would be famous?
No, I never thought he'd be famous. Every mother dreams about it I suppose, but you always think it happens to someone else.

What's your favourite Boyzone song?
I like 'Should Be Missing You Now', the second track on the 'Father and Son' single.

mumzone

MIKEY'S MUM, SHEILA GRAHAM

What was he like as a child?
He was noisy and full of devilment. He was always a little gangster.

Do you remember the day he was born?
I'll never forget it! It was a Tuesday at noon as the Angeles rang. I was all set for a delivery at home, but we had to send for an ambulance from the Rotunda when the baby started getting into distress.

Why did you call him Mikey?
My husband's only brother died in March of the year that Mikey was born and he was called Michael Christopher. We called him after his dad's brother but his grandfather was also the same name. We also put "Mary" in his name, in thanks for a safe delivery but I didn't actually put Mary on his birth certificate.

What were his favourite toys?
Dinky cars and a rocking horse that his dad made him. He also got a present of a rocking horse from Spain which he called Manuel. He loved that too. I think it's still in the attic.

Did he like school?
When he started he did because he loved the teacher. He was only six years old and he'd say she had lovely legs.

Was he ever in trouble?
He was always in trouble. I remember one day I got a phone call from the headmaster in St David's Primary School to get down to the school straight away and I thought he'd burned the place down. He and some other fellas were playing footsie, swinging off one of the sinks in the toilet when it fell off the wall.

The whole toilets and cloakroom were flooded. He got the blame on his own and he wouldn't tell who else was doing it with him. Of course, I had to pay the whole bill for the repairs out of my own pocket. But honestly from the tone of the phonecall I got from the headmaster I thought he'd burned the whole place to the ground. I didn't know what had happened! He was always giving me frights like that!

What were his hobbies?
He was really into the Billy Barry dancing school and he used to do tap dancing. He was also in the Boy Scouts and he did martial arts too.

What did he want to be when he grew up?
He told me he was going to be famous. He said he was going to make me rich and buy me a big house and a big car, and I have to say he has been very good to me.

Did you believe he was going to be famous?
Not at all! I used to say, "Good boy, you grow up and be famous. You've got the right attitude." But I never really thought that he would be.

What's your favourite Boyzone song?
'Working My Way Back to You.'

mumzone

mumzone

KEITH'S MUM, PAT DUFFY

What was his favourite toy?
Humpty Dumpty, a stuffed toy.

What was he like as a child?
He certainly wasn't a placid child. He was always very loveable though. He'd always give you a hug and he got everything going. He was always sick, he got whooping cough and then he got pneumonia out of that, and he had problems with his tonsils and then measles - and this was all before he was three! He was a very cuddly child though.

Did he like school?
Definitely not. The only thing he enjoyed was football.

What day was he born?
Tuesday.

Do you remember any funny incident when he was a child?
Keith was always one for saying, "my teacher says," and one day at Christmas when Keith was 6 and Derek was 9 they got a tape recorder. So, of course, they wanted to use the recorder and Keith as usual had to perform and he sang the Christmas carol, 'Silent Night'. When it got to the part "Round Yon Virgin Mother and Child", Keith sang "Brown John Virgin" and everyone started laughing. Keith immediately started with his "my teacher says". We still have the tape and we still get a laugh out of it.

What did he want to be when he grew up?
He wanted to be a footballer and play in Croke Park. When he was in Junior School he actually played in Croke Park for the finals of a football league, but they didn't win.

What were his hobbies?
Football, hurling and playing the drums, he was in a marching band.

Why did you call him Keith?
I used to babysit this cute baby called Keith and I suppose it always seemed like a nice name because of this baby.

Did you ever think he'd be famous?
I didn't, but my best friend always said he'd end up on stage. He was always a show person. He never liked being in the background. He was a real extrovert.

What's your favourite Boyzone song?
'When All Is Said And Done'.

mumzone

mumzone
AFAM
GURA

STEVE'S MUM, MARGARET GATELY

Why did you call him Steve?
There were already too many Paddys in the family. The Six Million Dollar Man used to be on the telly at that time and Steve Austen was his name. I thought he was gorgeous so I called him after the programme I suppose. His second name is Patrick.

What was his favourite toy?
Miss Piggy from the Muppets. He got it for his birthday. He always loved the show and even as a little baby he knew exactly when the show was on the telly.

What was he like as a child?
He was quiet, too quiet at times.

Did he like school?
He loved school. He was always excellent at school and he got on well with his teachers.

Do you remember the day he was born?
It was Wednesday, St Patrick's Day, and he arrived after just 30 minutes. He was the easiest baby in the world.

What did he want to be when he grew up?
He wanted to be a model or a singer. He used to dance to music before he was a year old. He loved it. He was so cute. He was a beautiful child. He did some modelling at Butlins when he was around twelve.

What were his hobbies?
He produced a play with the Walk to Talk drama group. He liked acting and performing.

Did you ever think he would be famous?
I always thought he'd be somebody. I knew he was going to do things. But I see his younger brother Tony playing football, and I think I'm going to see him playing team football on telly some day soon. All the boys have talent, Alan is good at art and Mark is very good in martial arts.

Do you remember a funny childhood incident with Steve?
I remember one day when he was only eight or nine when he came in from mass very upset. He told me he had dropped the collection box in the church and had to pick up all the money in front of everyone. "They were all laughing at me," he told me, and he said he'd never go back to the church again.

mumzone

RONAN'S MUM, MARIE KEATING

What was he like as a child?
He was very good as a baby. He was walking at ten months and was generally no trouble. He was a good child. I used to kill his brother Garry, but I never had to smack Ronan. He was a very sensitive child.

Do you remember any funny incidents when he was growing up?
I remember laughing so much one day when Ronan was about 6 and Garry was about 11. They came down from the bathroom where they were using their dad's razor and they had shaved off all the hair on their arms and legs. I told them they'd turn into gorillas with all the hair that would grow back and they got an awful fright. You'd should have seen their expressions, they were so worried. I really laughed at the state of them. Garry was always leading Ronan into some devilment and Ronan always wanted to be like his older brother.

What were his favourite toys?
With Ronan it was always toy cars and bicycles.

Did he like school?
He loved school, but he hated homework.

What day was he born on?
Thursday.

What were his hobbies growing up?
His mountain bike and he was mad into computers.

What did he want to be when he grew up?
He wanted to be a policeman. But I think that was only so he could ride a motorbike. He was just always car mad.

Did you ever think he would be famous?
No, I didn't. But a friend of mine that worked in the hairdressing salon with me said she remembers him coming in and looking at himself in the mirror and telling us, "One day I'll be famous."

What's your favourite Boyzone song?
'Should be Missing You Now.'

quizone

How well do you know the Boyz?
Check out the questions below and find out.
Answers at the bottom of page 27.

1. Which eyebrow does Shane shave?
2. What colour are Ronan's eyes?
3. Who is Steve's favourite singer?
4. Which member of the group was injured while horse riding?
5. What is Mikey's full name?
6. Which two members of Boyzone are dads?
7. Which member of the group has a ghost in his house?
8. What was Mikey's job before he joined the group?
9. Who is Steve's favourite actress?
10. Who used to work in a shoe shop?
11. Which member of Boyzone appeared in a TV advert before he joined the group?
12. Which American boy group first had a hit with 'Love Me For A Reason'?
13. What was Shane's favourite boy band when he was a kid?
14. Which of the Boyz has a Tasmanian devil tatooed on his hip?
15. What are Steve's favourite puppets?
16. Which of the Boyz won the BMX Championships in Ireland at the age of 14?
17. Who is the tallest member of the group?
18. What has Shane tatooed on his shoulder?
19. Which of the Boyz is the oldest?
20. Which member of the group wrote 'Together'?
21. Who is Ronan's favourite singer?
22. What is Steve's favourite TV show?
23. Which of the Boyz is especially good at catching up with fan mail?
24. Which of the Boyz once had a 'stick' hairstyle?
25. Is black hair Shane's natural colour?

e

answers

1. Right.
2. Blue.
3. Janet Jackson.
4. Mikey.
5. Michael Christopher Charles Graham.
6. Keith and Mikey.
7. Steve.
8. A mechanic.
9. Michelle Pfeiffer.
10. Ronan and Steve.
11. Mikey. He appeared in a TV advert for the Irish electricity board.
12. The Osmonds.
13. New Kids On The Block.
14. Steve.
15. Zig and Zag.
16. Shane.
17. Keith. He beats Shane by an inch.
18. A stallion.
19. Mikey.
20. Ronan.
21. George Michael.
22. Top Of The Pops.
23. Steve.
24. Shane.
25. No. It's brown.

ON THE COU

CH...SHANE

Do you believe in love at first sight? I believe in lust at first sight.

Did you ever date a girl older than you? Yes. When I was seventeen I got involved with the first real love of my life. She was 21.

Did you ever have a serious crush on a girl at school? Yes. Actually, it was one of my teachers. She was small and blonde. I don't think she knew that I fancied her.

Were you a model student? I thought I was, but the teachers didn't think so. One time when I got into trouble for swearing in class they told me not to come back the following term. So I didn't.

Are you close to your dad? Yeah. He's me best mate and we share a common passion for racing cars.

Did you ever have an experience with the supernatural? Yes. One time I was messing with an Ouija board and me and my sisters made contact with a girl from the other side. It was a really weird experience.

Are you a happy person? Very happy.

Would you be tempted to try drugs? No. I think anyone who does is mad. Drugs just mess you up.

Have you ever snogged more than one girl in a night? Yeah, I snogged three one night.

When did you think about becoming a pop star? When I saw New Kids On The Block. I had their posters on me bedroom wall.

What's your worst memory as a child? Hitting my dad in the eye with a golf club. It was an accident, but he had to be taken to hospital to get loads of stitches. I was horrified.

What's your bedroom like? It's black. Everything in it is black.

What's your ideal girl? A small girl with small breasts and dyed hair.

Would you ever consider having a serious relationship with a fan? I don't know. It all depends if I fell in love with someone.

How romantic are you? I'd give myself a four out of five. I think I treat girls well. But I'm not one for going out to dinner and showering a girl with presents.

How would you like to spend a special date? I'd like to go bungee jumping or parachuting, strapped together!

Do you have an inny or an outy belly button? An outy.

What was your most embarrassing moment? I was washing me car at a garage and a girl stopped across the road in her car. She waved over and as I waved back a guy came from behind me and walked over to her. She had been waving at him!

Do you believe in ghosts? Yeah.

What do you wear in bed? Boxers.

Have you got a hidden skill? I'm a mechanic.

Do you fear the future? No.

Stargazing... RONAN

Ronan's date of birth: 03/03/77

Steve's date of birth: 17/03/76

Star sign: Pisces

Element: Water

Key characteristics: Sensitive, selfless, sympathetic, mystical, modest
Key faults: Impressionable, weak-willed, lack of self-confidence, passive, pessimistic, vague

Pisces in profile

Pisceans are the least arrogant members of the zodiac. They tend to be gentle, shy, and modest and are more reluctant to take centre stage than other signs. Because of their mild manner they can often be shoved out of the spotlight by more forceful companions.

As Pisceans, Ronan and Steve are very sensitive souls. They're emotional, dreamy and romantic and although their sign is the fish, they're often inclined to have their head in the clouds. They are peaceful, warm and welcoming. Pisceans don't like to make waves and often end up being martyrs to the cause. They can also be a bit of a worrywart and some take a gloomy view of life.

Pisces in work

Being very non-competitive, Pisceans rarely climb to the top of the corporate ladder. Using feelings rather than logic, they can often drift through life without any positive aim or direction. Pisceans tend to be artistically and musically gifted and certainly Steve and Ronan are suited to this world.

Pisces in love

Pisceans make wonderfully caring partners. They have an endless supply of understanding and compassion. They are kind, sensitive, loving, sympathetic and always ready to help. They can be a bit clinging, but are devoted partners.

Ronan and Steve would make considerate boyfriends and would be generous with time, money and affection. Pisceans look for intimate, romantic partners.

WHAT THE STARS SAY ABOUT

& STEVE

Zodiac girls for Ronan and Steve...
As the retiring creatures of the zodiac, Ronan and Steve would be advised to team up with other Pisceans, Cancerians or Scorpios, which are also water signs.

Earth signs, Virgo, Taurus and Capricorn can also be a good match, although Taureans can sometime trample over Ronan or Steve's delicate feelings without even realising it.

Pisceans can be too clinging for the independent nature of air signs, such as Gemini, Aquarius and breezy Libra, and they will be totally overwhelmed by fiery fire signs, Sagittarius, Leo and Aries.

Ronan and the stars....
Do you read your horoscope every day?
If I see it in a magazine or paper I'll always have a look at it, but I don't go looking for my horoscope.

Does this profile of Pisces resemble you in any way?
It's exactly me and it's funny but Steve is very similar too. I wouldn't say I'm terribly pessimistic, but I am always being accused of having my head stuck in the clouds.

Do you believe in star signs and horoscopes?
After reading this I do!

Steve and the stars ....
Do you read your horoscope every day?:
I think it's a bit of fun, so if I see my horoscope in the paper, I'll always read it.

Does this profile of Pisces resemble you in any way?
It's very like me, although I wouldn't consider myself terribly shy or quiet anymore, but I was when I was younger.

Do you believe in star signs and horoscopes?
Yes, sort of. Ronan and myself are quite similar and we're the same sign. But Mikey, for example, is the complete opposite to us in real life and as a Leo he is the complete opposite in the zodiac.

Other famous Pisceans

Elizabeth Taylor
Prince Andrew
Prince Edward
Jasper Carrott
Jilly Cooper
Bruce Forsyth
Frankie Howerd
Dennis Waterman

boyz want to meet

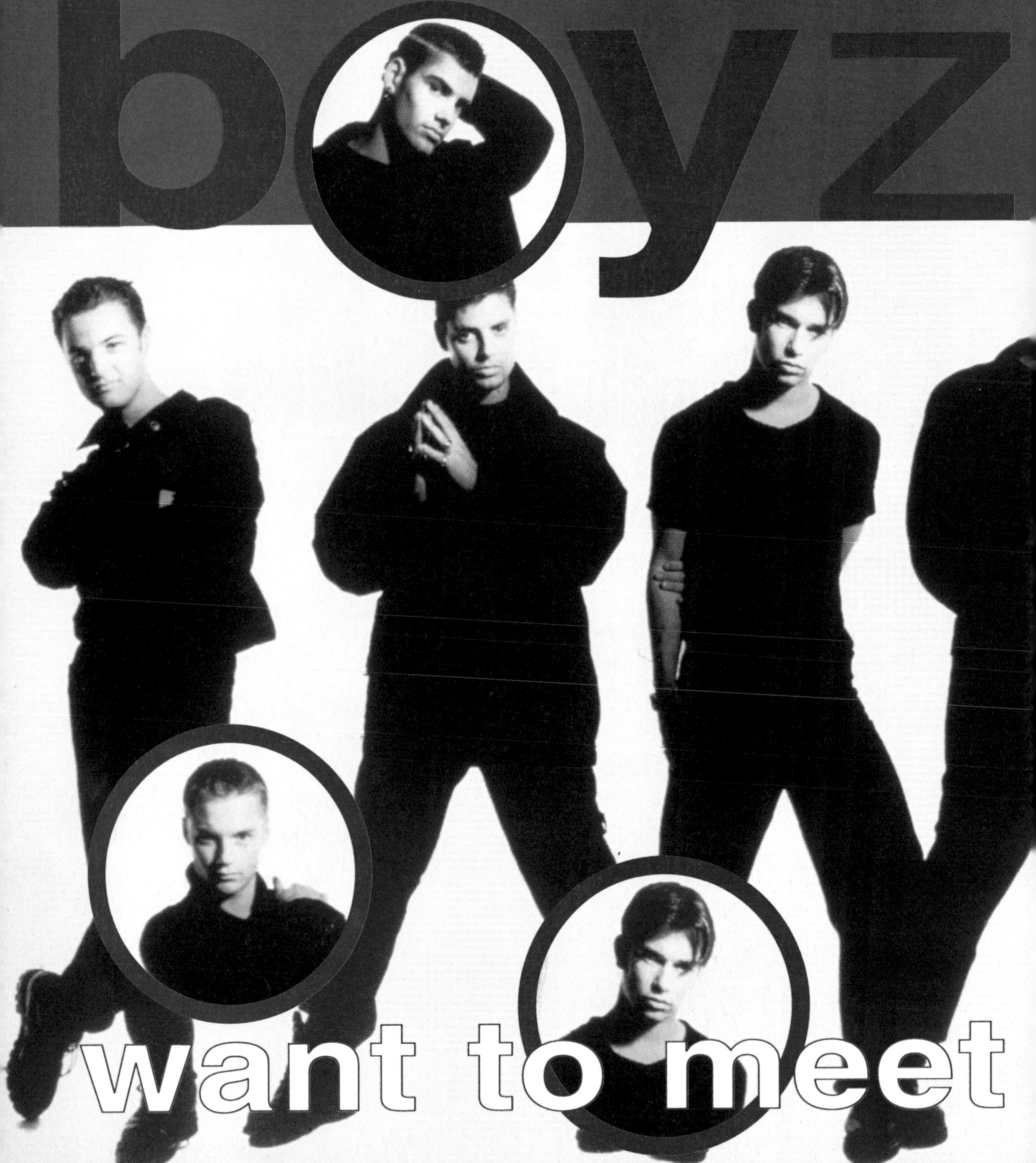

Yes, the five pin-up hunks have agreed to allow YOU and a pal into their inner sanctum.

It's the chance of a lifetime to get up close to the Boyz and find out what they're really like.

one

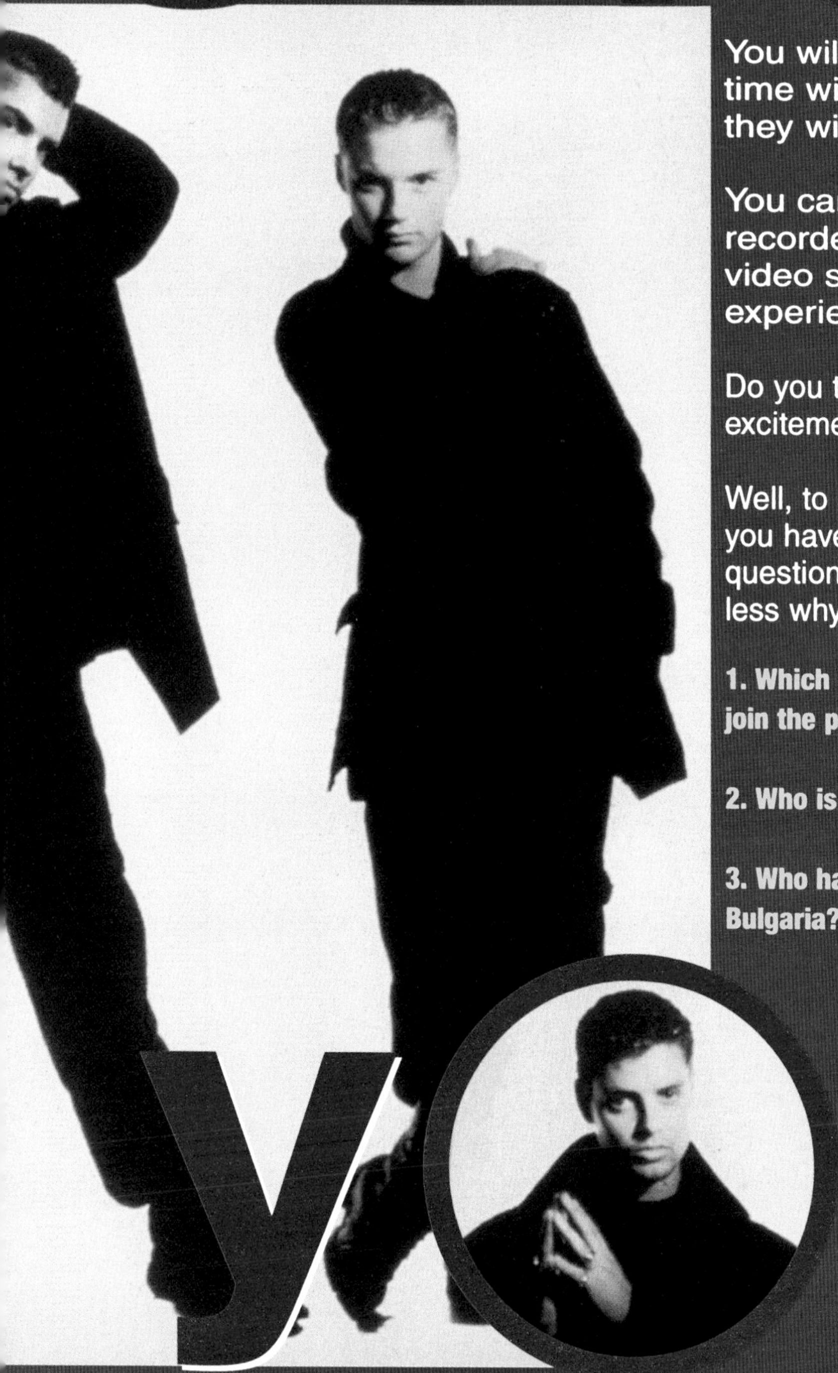

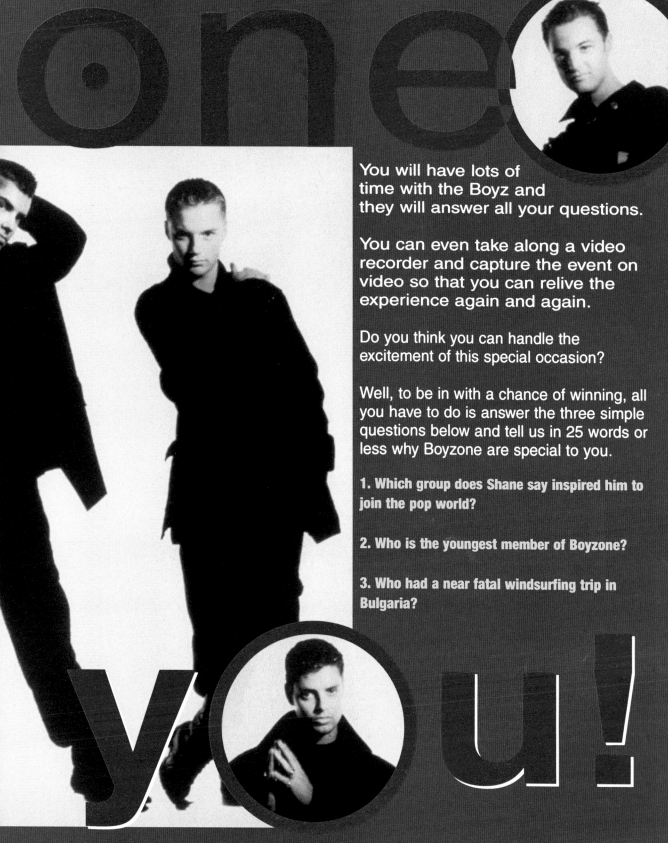

You will have lots of time with the Boyz and they will answer all your questions.

You can even take along a video recorder and capture the event on video so that you can relive the experience again and again.

Do you think you can handle the excitement of this special occasion?

Well, to be in with a chance of winning, all you have to do is answer the three simple questions below and tell us in 25 words or less why Boyzone are special to you.

1. Which group does Shane say inspired him to join the pop world?

2. Who is the youngest member of Boyzone?

3. Who had a near fatal windsurfing trip in Bulgaria?

you!

Write your answers on a postcard, or the back of a sealed down empty envelope, including your name, age and address, and post to:

Boyzone Competition
Grandreams Limited
Jadwin House, 205-211 Kentish Town Road, London NW5 2JU

Closing date for entries is 31st March 1997. The publishers' decision is final and no correspondence will be entered into.

ON THE COU

CH... MIKEY

What's your worst feature? Me face (laughs).

What's your best feature? My right hook!

Do you have an inny or outy belly button? An inny.

Are you a happy person? Generally.

What's your most embarrassing moment? On stage at the Smash Hits show and realising that my flies were open.

What do you wear in bed? Shorts.

When did you last cry? When my baby was born.

Did you have a formal sex education? I learned it from my pals first, but we did at one stage get sex education at school.

Was your first sexual experience memorable or disappointing? It was a whole new experience. It was interesting.

Did you ever have a near death experience? Twice. Once in Bulgaria when a storm blew up as I was windsurfing. It swept me out to sea and I had to dump the sail and paddle back to shore. On another occasion I was thrown off my bicycle when a motorist opened a car door. I landed in the path of a bus and narrowly escaped being run over.

Do you spend long grooming yourself? No. I just do the basics...fix my hair and then I'm out the door.

Do you remember your first kiss? Yes. She was an English visitor to my area. I was eight and she was 10.

How many kids would you like to have? Eight.

What do you do when you're feeling miserable? I just go off on my own and work my way through it. I always want to be alone when I'm miserable.

Are you a big drinker? Nah, not really. I do drink, but I don't get completely out of it. I like to be in control.

Have you ever had a supernatural experience? No. But I believe in heaven and hell and I believe that how you behave while you're on earth affects you in the next world.

Do you do your own housework? When I'm on tour there are people who look after all those things, but I do my own ironing and stuff when I'm home.

Do you think you're a tough guy? Well, I don't go around looking for trouble, but I could handle myself in a situation.

Have you a hidden skill? I'm a mechanic and superb guitar player.

How romantic are you? I'd give myself five out of five. I've always treated ladies the way a lady should be treated.

How would you like people to regard you? As a good, loyal friend...a nice person that they can trust.

What does love mean to you? I don't think anyone understands what love really means.

Have you ever had your heart broken? Oh yeah, a couple of times. I think that's something everyone experiences. It's all part of growing up and developing as a person.

Do you fear the future? Yeah, because you never know what's going to happen to you.

We asked the Boyz to give us a selection of their Top 10 favourites.

the zone

Mikey
Album: 'Jagged Little Pill' Alanis Morissette
Song: 'Demolition Man' Sting
Movie: The Godfather
Game: Frustration
Aftershave: Herrera
Item of clothing: Jeans
Toy: Car
Item jewellery: A Patriot ring
Holiday: Bermuda
Sport: Boxing

Keith
Album: 'Older' George Michael
Song: 'True Colours' Cyndi Lauper
Movie: Point Break
Game: Dominoes
Aftershave: Hugo Boss
Item of clothing: Sweatshirt
Hobby: Driving
Jewellery: A ring I have on a necklace
Holiday: Caribbean cruise
Sport: Gaelic football and hurling

Shane
Album: 'Bag Of Rhythm' UB40
Song: 'Unchained Melody' The Righteous Brothers
Movie: Bad Boys
Book: Don't have one
Aftershave: Don't use it
Item of clothing: Baggy trousers
Hobby: Cars
Item of jewellery: All my jewellery
Holiday: Portugal
Sport: Motor racing

Ronan
Album: 'Older' George Michael
Song: 'Nobody Knows' Tony Rich Project
Movie: Hunt For Red October
Aftershave: Sculpture
Item of clothing: Track suit bottoms
Hobby: Cars
Jewellery: A white gold ring
Holiday: America
Sport: Motor racing

Steve
Album: 'Les Miserables'
Song: 'Killing Me Softly' Fugees
Movie: Sister Act 2
Book: The Weirdstone of Brisingham
Aftershave: Eternity
Fashion store: Brown Thomas (Dublin)
Hobby: Sailing
Item of jewellery: My watch
Holiday: Disneyland
Sport: Badminton

Boyz motto

Be nice to everyone on the way up because you're going to meet them again on the way down.

Food corner

They say the way to a boy's heart is through his tummy. If you want to impress the Boyz in the kitchen, here's what they like:

Ronan: Lots of pasta.
Steve: Breast of chicken curry.
Shane: Lobster.
Mikey: Breast of chicken with sweetcorn.
Keith: Cabbage, bacon, mashed potatoes and loads of butter.

Super human

When you become a pop star do you change into a special person? "Oh no," says Keith. "I always thought that famous people were something special. Now that we're famous we're still just the same as we always were."

Tattoo crazy

Boyzone love tattoos. Here's a guide to the Boyz body work

Ronan: "I have a Japanese symbol which means warrior. I never had any interest in tattoos, but now I love my own. It's pretty neat."

Steve: "Mine is a Tasmanian Devil. I had it done without telling me mam. She doesn't really like them, but she's got used to it now. But I think one is enough."

Shane: "I love tattoos and I've had two done already. One is a stallion and the other is Japanese writing which means friendship. The stallion hurt really bad when I was getting it done because it's near the bone. I'll probably get more."

Keith: "I love tattoos and I've had two done. One is on my right arm and the other, a panther, is one my right shoulder blade. I'm going to get more done."

Phone Zone:

All the Boyz, except Keith, have a mobile phone. Who are they calling?

Steve: "I call my sister the most. We're very close. I wouldn't go anywhere without my phone. It keeps me close to the ones I love. In the early days the other guys in the group used to call me ET because I always had to phone home!"

Ronan: "I always call me mam. A day never passes that I don't talk to her on the phone."

Shane: "I call home and there's a few friends that I keep in touch with regularly."

Mikey: "I call my family and my girlfriend. I look forward to the day that I'll be able to talk to my little daughter on the phone."

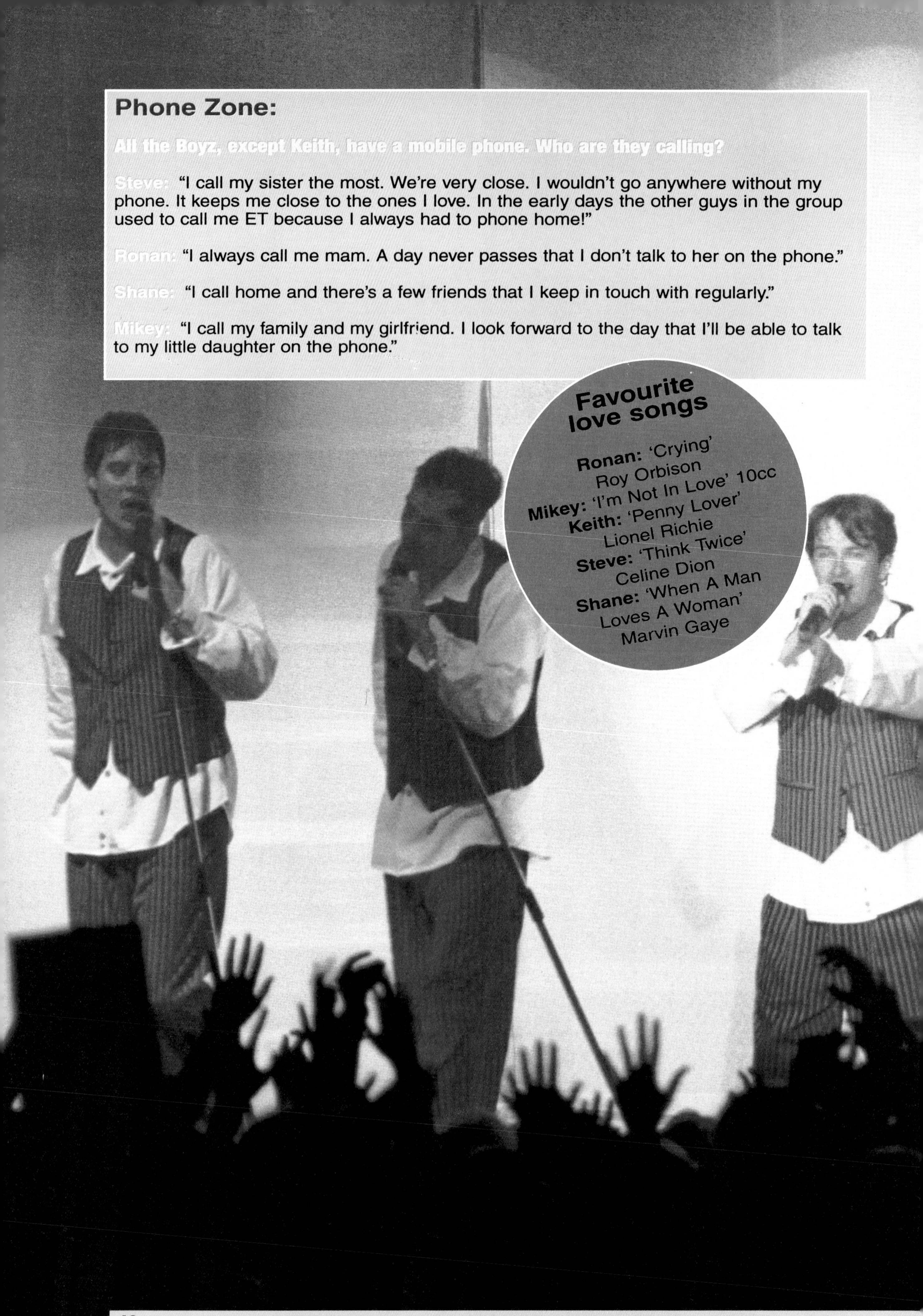

Favourite love songs

Ronan: 'Crying' Roy Orbison

Mikey: 'I'm Not In Love' 10cc

Keith: 'Penny Lover' Lionel Richie

Steve: 'Think Twice' Celine Dion

Shane: 'When A Man Loves A Woman' Marvin Gaye

What day were you born on?

Monday's child is fair of face
Tuesday's child is full of grace (**Mikey & Keith**)
Wednesday's child is loving and giving (**Steve**)
Thursday's child works hard for a living (**Ronan**)
Friday's child is full of woe
Saturday's child has far to go (**Shane**)
But the child that is born on the **Sabbath** day
is bonny and blithe and bright and gay

Boyzone Birthstones:

Ronan
Born: 03/03/77
Birthstones: Crystal, Aquamarine and Emerald

Steve
Born: 17/03/76
Birthstones: Crystal, Aquamarine and Emerald

Shane
Born: 03/07/76
Birthstones: Pearl and Moonstone

Keith
Born: 03/07/76
Birthstones: Sapphire and Opal

Mikey
Born: 15/08/72
Birthstones: Ruby and Amber

Scar zone

Ronan has lots of scars including six(!) on his head from a rock falling on him, one on his left arm from a burn, one on his right arm from a knife and two on his forehead.

Car crazy

Four of the Boyz are fast car fanatics. Ronan has a BMW. Shane has a Porsche 911. Mikey owns a Mazda sports car and Keith has an Escort XR3i.

Ronan plastered

Ronan occasionally wears a plaster on his index finger as a lucky mascot.

Names

All the names of the Boyz have a special meaning. We investigate:

Keith:

Keith is a Scottish surname and placename meaning 'a wood'. It wasn't used as a first name until this century. Other Gaelic translations say the name Keith means 'the wind'.

Ronan:

Ronan is the name of a fifth-century Irish saint and means 'little seal'. The female version of Ronan is Rowena or the more modern, Rhona or Rona.

Shane:

Shane comes from the name Sean which is Gaelic for 'John'. This name comes from Hebrew and means 'the Lord is gracious'. It has remained one of the most popular names for boys since the early middle ages. The Scots translated the name as Ian or Jock, the Welsh as Iwan, Ifan, Evan or Ewen, and the Irish as Sean or Eoin.

Steve:

Steve is a pet name of Stephen which comes from the Greek word 'crown". Saint Stephen was the first person to be martyed for his Christian faith. He was stoned to death after accusing Jewish Elders of rejecting the true God. St Stephen's feast day is December 26, the day on which King Wenceslas looked out and saw the poor man gathering winter fuel. Wenceslas is a central European name usually found as Vaclav or Wenzel and shares the same meaning for Stephen translating in Slavic languages as 'crown' and 'glory'.

Mikey:

Mikey is a pet name of Michael which comes from the Hebrew for 'Who is like God?' It also appears in the Old Testament in the form of the name of the prophet Micah. The popularity of the Archangel Michael, who defeated Satan, spread the name throughout Europe. It also became a surname in the form of Mitchel.

Ronan on fans: "Sometimes they scare me, especially when I'm on my own and I've got 400 of them running after me."

Keith on rude banners at Boyzone concerts: "It's funny to see rude ones. I can't remember any phrases off hand, but there was one about my broken teeth - it was really, really filthy dirty, what they'd like to do with my broken teeth."

Steve on the person he'd most like to snog: "I'd like to snog Janet Jackson. She just looks really, really soft."

Mikey on showbiz parties: "I don't like them because there's very often a lot of pretentious people hanging out there."

Keith on his favourite Boyzone moment: "Being on stage and performing."

Mikey on the question of fame going to his head: "It's not a pretty thing to see fame change someone. It's like they're cheating themselves out of who they are. I've never caught myself going over the top. I've always tried to be myself no matter who I'm talking to."

Talkzone

The Boyz fill acres of space in magazines through interviews all year round. Here we check out what they've been saying.

Keith on how much it would take for him to pose nude in a magazine: "I wouldn't do it for less than £50,000."

Ronan on English fans: "The English fans are a lot older than back home, but they scream just as loudly."

Shane on what he'd do if he saw a good looking girl in the crowd: "I'd go check her out. Probably introduce myself."

Ronan on his favourite smell: "I love the smell of fresh flowers. I love the smell of new cut grass, that's gorgeous too."

Steve on getting presents: "I don't get as many as I used to, probably because all the girls who wanted to give me presents have done so by now."

Mikey on who'll be the first to leave Boyzone: "I don't know. If we start to go down we'll all go together."

Ronan on whether he's the sexiest guy in the group: "I don't think so. Shane is the sexiest."

Steve on whether he finds older women attractive: "Oh yeah, definitely. Someone like Michelle Pfeiffer."

Keith on being a pop star: "I'm in a famous pop group but I'm not one of the main singers so I don't see myself as a pop star. I'm not one of the favourites, I'm one of the numbers. It's more Ronan, Steve and Shane that are really the favourites."

Steve on how he has changed since joining Boyzone: "I've become a lot wiser to people. I'm not as trusting as I was. I don't have much trust for people now, which is sad."

Shane on how they behave when their parents are at a Boyzone concert: "There's a lot of things you wouldn't do on stage when they're there. Not that you're not yourself, but you're more aware of what you do."

Mikey on his favourite fruit: "It's passion fruit, 'cause there's passion involved with eating it and once you've tasted it you're hooked for life."

Keith on what he misses on tour: "Having a shower in the morning. When you're on a bus you can't fall out of bed and into a shower."

Ronan on his favourite part of Dublin: "Me bedroom. Me house. I don't have a favourite part, just my house."

Mikey on whether or not he'd be able to beat Oasis star Liam Gallagher in a fight: "I wouldn't be afraid of him by any means. I've boxed against harder than him."

Ronan on his favourite sleeping position: "I lie flat on my stomach and I don't have a pillow. I hate pillows. If there is a pillow, I put it halfway over my head. My head has to be flat when I'm sleeping."

Keith on his looks: "I think I was much better looking when I was younger. I had a lot more character. I used to have long blond hair. I got big-headed when I was younger because I was really popular, then I got a bad dose of acne for two years."

Ronan on being a dad: "I'd love to be a dad. I love kids. I have a nephew called Conal. I'm his godfather and I love him to bits. He's cool."

ON THE COU

CH...STEVE

Do you remember your first day at school? Yeah. I screamed my head off. It was a very emotional experience being parted from my mum. It's terrible what little kids have to go through.

Were you a model student? Yeah, but one day the teacher wouldn't let me go to the toilet and I went in my pants. I didn't do it on purpose. I just couldn't hold it in any longer.

Did you ever have a job outside Boyzone? Yeah, I worked in a bar and in a shoe shop.

How old were you when you had your first kiss? I was 12. That girl still sends me cards for my birthday and at Christmas.

How many children would you like to have? Two. A boy and a girl.

Would you ever try drugs? No way. I've seen what they do to people and it's terrifying.

Did you ever have an experience with the supernatural? Yeah. There's a ghost in our house and I've seen him many times. It scares the hell out of me.

Do you believe in evil spirits? Yeah. I wear a precious stone around my neck to keep them away.

Would you go out with a fan? Yeah, if she was the right fan. If she was really nice and really genuine, then I probably would.

What was your most embarrassing moment? I used to do the collection in church and one Sunday I dropped all the money during Mass and had to pick it all up.

What are the features that attract you to a girl? Teeth, lips and eyes.

What's your favourite book? 'The Enchanted Wood' by Enid Blyton.

Do you have any childhood toys left? I still have several muppets.

What bad habit really gets up your nose? Smoking.

What's you worst feature? Everything. Me.

What's your best feature? People say my lips and eyes.

Do you have an inny or an outy belly button? An inny.

Are you a happy person? Very happy.

What do you wear in bed? Boxers.

What do you do last thing at night? Brush my teeth.

What do you do first thing in the morning? Brush my teeth.

What's your biggest fear? Falling from a height on stage.

When did you last cry? A couple of nights ago because I was sad.

What is your most frightening dream? Falling and not finding anything to grab on to.

Have you got a hidden skill? Art.

Is there anyone else you would like to be? No. I'm happy with myself.

What was your happiest moment in life? Getting into Boyzone.

What was your saddest moment in life? I've had a few where people close to me died.

How did you feel the first time you performed on stage? I got off the stage and nearly collapsed.

Do you fear the future? No.

china b

The system of Chinese horoscopes has been around for thousands of years. Let's see what we can learn about the Boyz from the wisdom of the East.

Ronan - THE SNAKE

Ronan was born: 03/03/77
Chinese horoscope: The year of the Snake
Snake characteristics: Cautious, prudish, mysterious, wise and clever
Meaning of the sign: Wisdom

Snake Personality

Being born in the year of the Snake, Ronan is likely to be a wise person. Snakes are the serious thinkers of the Chinese horoscope. These are the deep thinkers. Their advice is usually worth listening to.

However, Snakes are quite unpredictable. They can be treacherous. Like their sign they are slippery creatures!

Mystery always surrounds the Snake person. Many have great spirituality and may be interested in religion. There is also much sensitivity in the Snake too, and arts and music usually play an important part in their lives.

Snakes are very good looking, and both male and female of the sign have elegant and stylish taste in clothes. As a result, they are often labelled vain. Males of the sign could not usually be described as butch. These are the 'New Men' of the horoscope!

Were you born in the year of the pig or the rat? Or perhaps you're a dragon, a monkey, a dog or a rabbit? What year were the Boyz born in?

CALENDER OF THE CHINESE HOROSCOPE

1970	6 Feb 1970 - 26 Jan 1971	DOG	1984	2 Feb 1984 - 19 Feb 1985	RAT
1971	27 Jan 1971 - 15 Jan 1972	PIG	1985	20 Feb 1985 - 8 Feb 1986	OX
1972	16 Jan 1972 - 2 Feb 1973	RAT	1986	9 Feb 1986 - 28 Jan 1987	TIGER
1973	3 Feb 1973 - 22 Jan 1974	OX	1987	29 Jan 1987 - 16 Feb 1988	RABBIT
1974	23 Jan 1974 - 10 Feb 1975	TIGER	1988	17 Feb 1988 - 5 Feb 1989	DRAGON
1975	11 Feb 1975 - 30 Jan 1976	RABBIT	1989	6 Feb 1989 - 26 Jan 1990	SNAKE
1976	31 Jan 1976 - 17 Feb 1977	DRAGON	1990	27 Jan 1990 - 14 Feb 1991	HORSE
1977	18 Feb 1977 - 6 Feb 1978	SNAKE	1991	15 Feb 1991 - 3 Feb 1992	SHEEP
1978	7 Feb 1978 - 27 Jan 1979	HORSE	1992	4 Feb 1992 - 22 Jan 1993	MONKEY
1979	28 Jan 1979 - 15 Feb 1980	SHEEP	1993	23 Jan 1993 - 9 Feb 1994	ROOSTER
1980	16 Feb 1980 - 4 Feb 1981	MONKEY	1994	10 Feb 1994 - 30 Jan 1995	DOG
1981	5 Feb 1981 - 24 Jan 1982	ROOSTER	1995	31 Jan 1995 - 18 Feb 1996	PIG
1982	25 Jan 1982 - 12 Feb 1983	DOG	1996	19 Feb 1996 - 7 Feb 1997	RAT
1983	13 Feb 1983 - 1 Feb 1984	PIG	1997	8 Feb 1997 - 27 Jan 1998	OX

Keith - THE TIGER

Keith was born: 01/10/74
Chinese horoscope: The year of the Tiger
Tiger characteristics: Dynamic, energetic, competitive, active, loud, upfront

Tiger Personality

As a Tiger, Keith likes to be in charge. Unlike the Ox who was born the year before him, Tigers never wait quietly on the sidelines, but always like to take centre stage. Taking orders is impossible for them and they tend to make up their own rules as they go along.

Dealing with red tape and dotting the 'I's' and crossing the 'T's' is not a Tiger's style. They have a very casual attitude to life.

As a Tiger, one of Keith's most outstanding qualities is courage. Tigers are fearless. They also have great energy that sweeps everyone along.

They are great flirts and are very passionate. Their magnetic personality attracts people like bees to honey, but tempermentally Tigers can be ferocious and hot-headed. They are known for having a very short fuse. However, apart from that, Tigers like Keith are very likeable people and will always have a wide following.

Mikey - THE RAT

Mikey was born: 15/08/72
Chinese horoscope: The year of the Rat
Rat characteristics: Amusing, witty, charming, sociable, pompous
Meaning of the sign: Charm

Rat Personality
The Chinese horoscope begins with the year of the Rat, so those born in this year like to be first. They like to lead the action. They see themselves as a cut above the rest - the creme de la creme. They thrive in situations that they can be looked up to.

Rats like Mikey are busy people. Challenge is essential and they like to live dangerously. Above all they hate dull routine. They are best known for their charm and sense of humour which can make them great company.

Rats are known to be very loyal to people they love and to their friends. However, when faced with difficulties or when they are unhappy, they become irritatingly fussy, fretting and niggling over silly details.

Generally though, as a Rat, Mikey is a lucky person with quick wits and a sense of fun that will ensure that he gets as much as possible out of life.

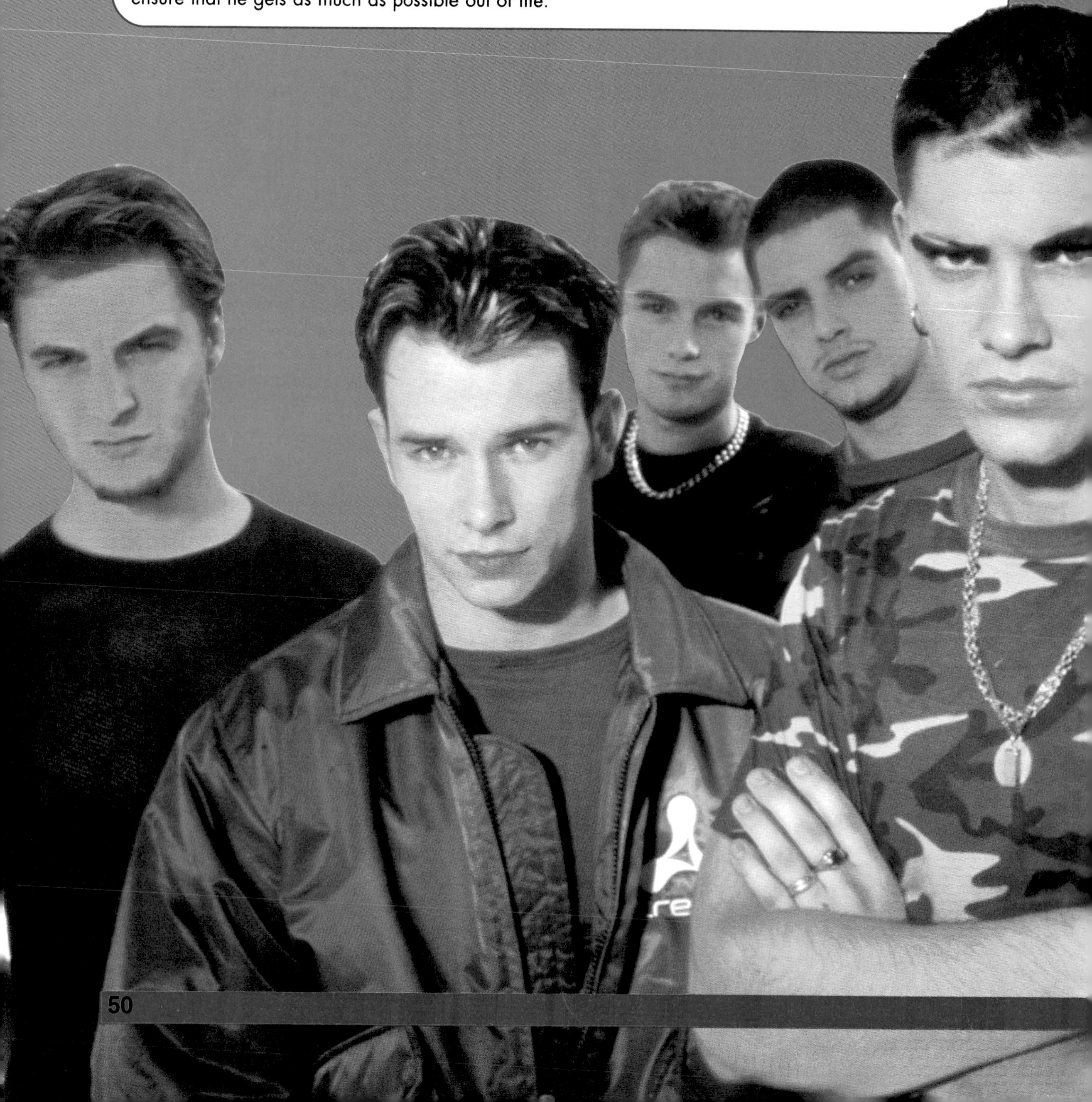

Shane and Steve - THE DRAGON

Shane was born: 03/07/76
Steve was born: 17/03/76
Chinese horoscope: The year of the Dragon
Dragon characteristics: Refined, self-assured, full of life, unusual, superficial
Meaning of the sign: Good luck and fortune

Dragon Personality

As Dragons, Steve and Shane are quite a hit with the girls. They are easy going and fit in with what goes on around them, but only as long as it suits them. They don't like being bossed and when they are, they can be as ferocious and dangerous as the mythical beast upon which the sign is based.

They are happiest in positions of power because they like to be in charge. Toeing the line is not easy for these creatures.

They are usually clever, bright people. No matter what happens Dragons will always land on their feet. This is due to the fact that those born in the year of the Dragon are the luckiest of all the signs and good fortune follows them wherever they go. The year of the Dragon is also good for all money-making schemes, so Shane and Steve should always attract money.

In general this sign is very popular without working at it. They bring a little magic and a bit of glamour wherever they go!

Stargazing...

Shane's date of birth: 03/07/76

Star sign: Cancer

Element: Water

Key characteristics: Sensitive, kind, compassionate, caring, loves security and stability, homebirds

Key faults: Over-cautious, moody, clinging, unforgiving, possessive

WHAT THE STARS SAY ABOUT

SHANE

Cancer in profile

Cancerians are the homebirds of the zodiac. Family ties are very important and they are often very close to their mothers. The word which best describes Cancer is sensitive.

As a Cancerian, Shane is very caring, kind and gentle. He would be protective as well as possessive. Cancerians also hold grudges like no-one else and will never forgive and forget. They are often prone to moodiness, and life with Shane could be a rollercoaster of emotional highs and lows.

Cancerians tend to be very conventional at heart and may follow traditional roles of 'Me Tarzan, You Jane' in the home. They are certainly not known for being 'new men'!

Cancer in work

Home and family is so important to Cancerians that they are often unhappy to follow work that brings them away from home. Many end up in jobs they can do from home and many of them are in their element in the kitchen. Many in this sign end up as chefs and cooks.

Cancer in love

Home-loving Cancerians only really thrive when they are in a warm, secure and loving relationship. They are very emotional and sensitive people who form very deep bonds with those they fall in love with. They are warm and cuddly partners who adore romance.

Shane can appear quite shy when meeting people of the opposite sex, but once he falls in love he gives everything to the relationship. When a Cancerian falls in love, it's forever.

Other famous Cancerians

Prince William

Bill Cosby

Meryl Streep

Donald Sutherland

Mel Brooks

Barbara Cartland

Sue Lawley

Zodiac girls for Shane

Being a water sign, Cancerians should avoid fire signs, Sagittarius, Aries and Leo like the plague. When the temperature is right, fire and water produce steam power, but all too often, too much fire will evaporate fire, and too much water will see a fire disappear. Fellow emotional water signs Scorpio and Pisces are probably the safest bet.

Shane and the stars

Do you read your horoscope every day?

I wouldn't deliberately go looking for my horoscope, but I'll always look at it if I come across it in the paper.

Does this profile of Cancer resemble you in any way?

My mother would say it did! I'm a real homebird, but I'm not the only one who gets homesick when we're away and I'm the only Cancerian in the group! I am quite shy and I've been accused of being a bit moody, although I wouldn't really say I am.

Do you believe in star signs and horoscopes?

I wouldn't say no, because there seems to be something to it, but I don't take it very seriously either.

	Keith	Ronan
What do you carry in your pockets?	Me wallet. It contains all types of things. There are hundreds of business cards, photos of the baby and Lisa and lots of private and personal things.	Tissues and coins.
What's in your bathroom bag?	Shaving foam, gel, toothbrush, toothpaste and aftershave. No girlie creams.	Aftershave, deodorants, toothbrush, toothpaste, the usual stuff.
What clothes do you have in your wardrobe?	Old clothes, stage clothes. Loads and loads of Nike runners.	I have hundreds of clothes...jackets, coats and shirts. I also have hundreds of pairs of shoes because I used to work in a shoe shop.
What was your worst fashion buy?	A pinstripe suit I bought in Top Man. It was a horrible joke.	I bought a coat for £500 and only wore it once.
What was your best fashion buy?	A karate-style suit.	Track suit bottoms that I bought for £50. I never take them off.

Up C

an
pers

sked the Boyz to let us have

Shane	Steve	Mikey
My house keys, mobile phone, receipts and wallet.	My wallet and keys.	Money, car keys, wallet.
The usual stuff and a pair of tweezers.	Apart from the usual things, there are cleansers, toners, moisturisers and special shampoos.	The usual stuff, shampoo, toothbrush, toothpaste, razor, etc.
Lots of different gear. I'm a clothes freak.	There are piles and piles of clothes. There is no room in the wardrobe and I have to put some of them on the bed.	Too many clothes. The most unusual is a pair of black furry trousers.
I have good taste in clothes.	A multi-coloured shirt.	Too many things to mention.
Nothing stands out.	A cream mac with big collars.	Hugo Boss suit.

lose

d

onal

peek inside their personal areas.

Red alert!

What colours reveal about the Boyz...

Roses are red,
Violets are blue,
And your favourite colour tells a lot about you!

...And so do some of the hues you hate! Psychologists say colours can tell a lot about your personality. So we gave a colour chart to the Boyz and asked them to choose their favourite and their least favourite colours. Here's what their choices say about their personalities:

STEVE

Favourite colour: Purple
Purple lovers tend to be rather unconventional. Purple is an unusual colour because it's made from two contradicting colours: red and blue. While red is stimulating, blue is relaxing.

Those who are attracted to purple are highly creative people with strong spiritual sides. A person who likes purple tends to be very individualistic without being a show off.

Hollywood's eccentric actor, Nicholas Cage, for example is a well known purple lover. So much so, his wife Patricia Arquette, presented him with a purple wedding cake on their wedding day.

Least favourite colour: Green
Green is an uplifting colour which is all about soothing and relaxing people. The person who hates green tends to be the sort of person who doesn't follow the crowd. They avoid thinking, looking or doing things the same way as most people. Green haters are the type to stand out from the crowd although they don't deliberately try to draw attention to themselves - they're just naturally different!

Steve says: "Can picking two colours really reveal all this? I liked purple on the chart you showed me, but I wouldn't be caught dead wearing it or anything. I actually like wearing black but that wasn't on the colour chart - what would that say about me? I have to say what the two colours have revealed seems quite accurate."

SHANE

Favourite colour: Green
Green is an uplifting colour. It relieves depression, and soothes and relaxes the mind and body. People who like green tend to be stable, kind and generous. They like taking things easy and generally enjoy a quiet life. Green lovers tend to be good friends. They are often easy to get on with and tend to have close, warm relationships with those around them.

Least favourite colour: Yellow
Yellow is anything but mellow. It's an energising colour which increases the pulse rate of anyone it surrounds. Those who hate yellow tend to be very practical and down to earth. They tend to be

suspicious of new ideas and prefer to concentrate on things they know they can accomplish. They are naturally cautious and hate to be rushed into anything.

Shane says: "I just picked those colours off the top of my head but I suppose what they've revealed is quite true. I wouldn't say I'm very practical though or that I'm suspicious of new ideas. I just hate yellow because I think it's a garish colour especially for someone to wear. I don't think it suits anyone and I hate a room with yellow walls. Green is a much easier colour to be surrounded by, especially lighter shades."

RONAN

Favourite colour: Blue
Blue is a relaxing colour. It lowers blood pressure, heart rates and soothes the emotions. People who are attracted to blue are romantic, emotional types. Shades of blue tell us that you're cool and confident but also a little vulnerable. Blue lovers are also sensitive to the needs of others and deeply hurt when someone betrays them.

Least favourite colour: Purple
Purple haters tend to have a strong need for sincerity, honesty and lack of pretence in their lives. They like people to be upfront. They like clarity and hate complications. Purple haters usually exercise good judgement and make good critics.

Ronan says: "There's nothing there that I'd contradict. I've always liked blue - there's something quite calming about blue. Purple just strikes me as a bit too rich or sickly. But do liking or hating these colours really mean all this?"

MIKEY

Favourite colour: Orange
Orange is another stimulating colour. It comes from red and yellow mixed together and shares their energising characteristics. Orange is said to encourage appetite and to reduce fatigue. Orange lovers like to stand out from the crowd. They're adventurous and full of zest for life and packed with oodles of energy.

Least favourite colour: Blue
Blue is a relaxing colour which soothes those around it. Those who reject blue are usually restless and bored by routine. They crave excitement and new faces and places.They like to be on the move and like to be in the spotlight.

Mikey says: "My favourite colour in clothes is black but there's no black on this colour chart and I immediately went for orange. What does that say about me? I suppose black in its own way is quite a dramatic colour like orange. You won't fade into the background in either colour. Blue is just a bit boring. Yes, I like lively surroundings and I like going new places and seeing new faces, but at the same time I love being at home too."

KEITH

Favourite colour: Red
Red is the most stimulating shade in the colour chart. It excites and warms the body. Red surroundings increase heart rate and brain activity according to the psychologists. It's the favourite colour for people who are impulsive, active, competitive and daring. They like living life to the full. They like thrills and fast living. Red lovers are adventurous types who are virtually unshockable!

Least favourite colour: Pink
Pink is a soothing colour. It relaxes muscles, reduces aggression and anxiety, and encourages rest. It is a warm, cosy colour that softens its surroundings.

Those who hate pink enjoy lots of change in life. They are looking for thrills and new opportunities. They hate the quiet life and are always rushing past in the fast lane.

Keith says: "I don't really wear red but it's a colour that I'm still attracted to. If I see a girl in a red dress I tend to look twice - I think lots of guys do. It's a great colour for a sports car. Pink is a colour that annoys me. It's a real sissy, frilly colour. I suppose what the colours reveal is quite true. I like lots of activity. I get a buzz out of doing new and exciting things. I hate things staying the same and I get easily bored if they do."

fanzone

Close to the heart of the Boyzone empire is their fan club. Who better to talk to about the Boyz and their fans than the two people who run their clubs: Mike Hrano in London and Alyson Hannon in Dublin.

How often do you see the Boyz?
Mike: We keep in close contact and I see them as often as I need to. Obviously they live in Dublin so I don't see that much of them, but when they are playing here I make sure I get to see them and bring them up their latest mail and presents.

How did you become head of the Boyzone fan club?
Mike: I was a journalist and then I started running the East 17 fan club. Their manager said to me there is a new band called Boyzone who were having a hit with 'Love Me For A Reason' and I should talk to their manager Louis Walsh. I did and they checked me out and then appointed me head of the fan club.

What is the most unusual gift you've received for Boyzone?
Mike: There's so much stuff coming here all the time it's hard to keep track of it but at the moment a lovely casket for 'Baby's First Tooth' has arrived here and is engraved 'Jordan' for Keith's new baby.

Do you ever return gifts?
Mike: Sometimes we receive rings that have been passed down through a family or pieces that are family heirlooms and we always say thank you but we would send it back. I'm sure fans' parents would not be very pleased with them sending something like that away! Other times we get a birthday card for one of the Boyz and it has cash in it, which is really sweet, but we always send it back telling them Boyzone would rather they spend it on themselves.

How much mail do you get and do you reply to all of it?
Mike: It would be impossible to reply to all

of it. We do our best to go through the mail and pass on what we need to but we estimate we received around 200,000 pieces of mail and gifts in the last year.

How often do you see the Boyz?
Alyson: They drop in here quite often to pick up their mail and all their gifts. We sort it out first and then deal with what we can and pass on the rest to them. Steve is really good, he tries to write back as much as possible.

Do you censor the mail?
Alyson: If we come across really obscene letters we bin them, but obviously the mail is Boyzone's and we don't go through it all for them.

What is the most unusual gift you've received for Boyzone?
Alyson: It's not unusual but it's certainly strange - sometimes we receive girls' underwear and it's not always washed!

How did you become head of the Boyzone fan club?
Alyson: I worked with Boyzone's manager Louis Walsh a few years ago and he asked me to get involved with organising the fan club in Dublin.

Alyson and Mike give us their top ten list of gifts that are received at the fan club office:

1. Baby clothes and toys for Keith and Mikey's babies.

2. Teddies. "We get hundreds and hundreds of teddies," says Alyson.

3. Friendship bracelets.

4. Long letters and cards, especially birthday cards.

5. Compilation tapes of fans singing. Also taped messages for the band.

6. Loads of Disney and Casper goodies for Steve because he said once in an interview that he collected Disney.

7. Books.

8. Lucky charms and stones.

9. Baseball caps for Keith and Shane because they're photographed often wearing them.

10. Lots of drawings, especially of Ronan. "Ronan seems to be the easiest member to draw," says Alyson.

boyzone
Fan Club
PO Box 102
Stanmore
Middlesex
HA7 2PY

Stargazing...

Keith's date of birth: 01/10/74

Star sign: Libra

Element: Air

• • • • • • • • • • • •

Key characteristics: Social, outgoing, charming, lively mind, artistic, people-pleaser, strives for harmony

Key faults: lazy, extravagant, smarmy, insincere, indecisive

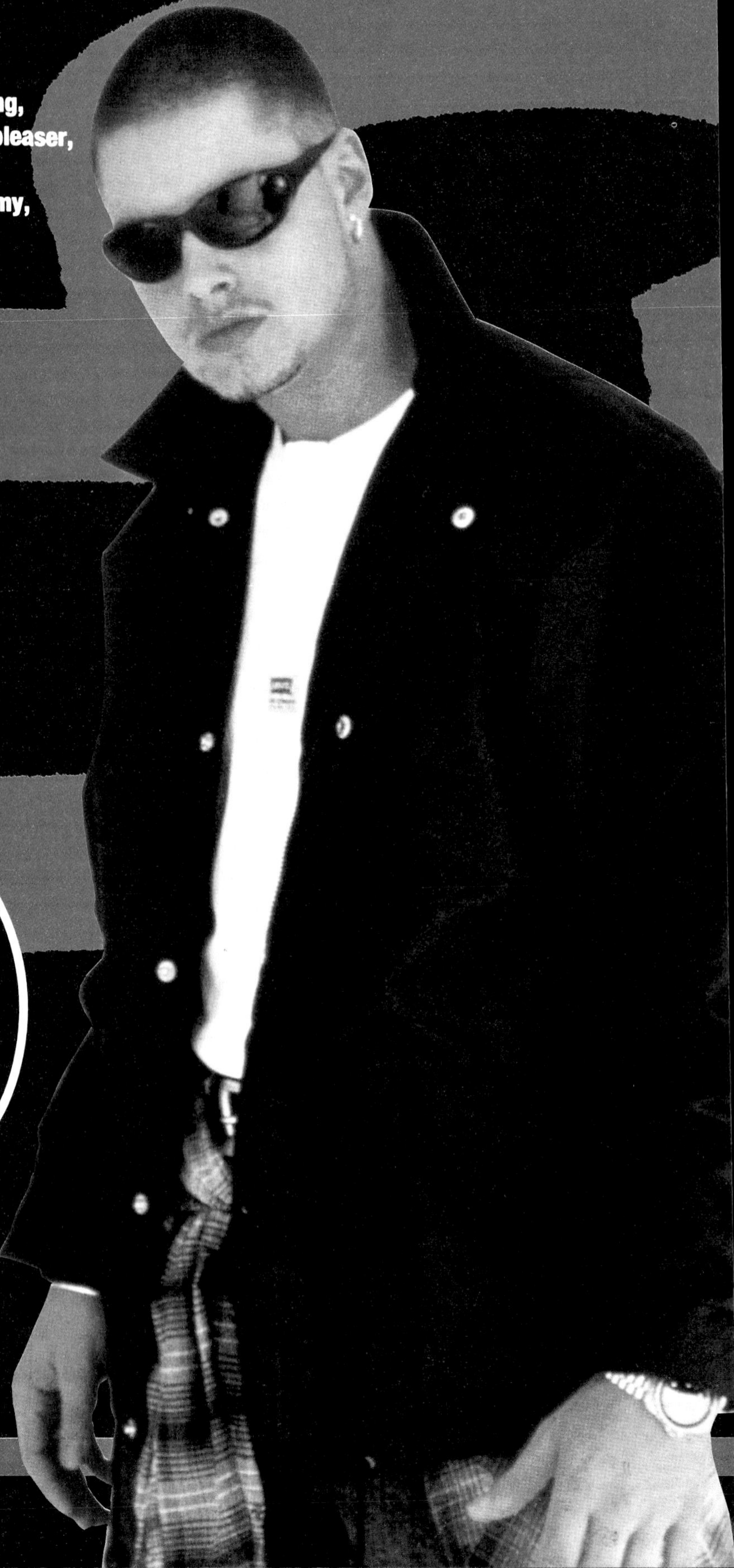

Other famous Librans

• • • • • • • •

Bruce Springsteen

Michael Douglas

Christopher Reeve

Olivia Newton-John

Brigitte Bardot

Julie Andrews

Gandhi

WHAT THE STARS SAY ABOUT

KEITH

Libra in profile

The scales is the symbol for Librans and those born under this sign like balance in their lives. Keith should have a great talent for seeing every side of an argument but unfortunately this often makes him a very poor decision maker.

Outwardly Librans are outwardly cool, calm and collected but their oodles of charm and tact can end up driving you mad.

Generally as a Libran, Keith loves all the beautiful things in life and surrounds himself with good food, good wine, good music, beautiful clothes and a good companion.

Libra in work

Keith's natural talent for peacemaking makes him perfect for a career in diplomacy. A Libran's love of beauty leads many to follow careers in the arts, music, fashion or design. Keith should make the perfect teammate as Librans thrive in work situations that involve teamwork.

Libra in love

Librans might have invented the notion of romance. They are one of the most romantic signs in the zodiac. They have the most difficulty staying alone and need a settled relationship to feel really happy.

When it comes to romance, it would be difficult to find a more pleasing partner that Keith. Librans are very romantic people and they often get swept away, falling in love with love itself, rather than truly falling head over heels for another person. They very easily become infatuated.

Other famous Libreans

Bob Geldof

Charlton Heston

Britt Ekland

John Lennon

Roger Moore

Pavarotti

Sting

Zodiac girls for Keith

Libra is an air sign and gets on best with the other air signs, Gemini and Aquarius. Fire signs Leo and Sagittarius are also favourable partners.

Keith and the stars

Do you read your horoscope every day?

No, I never look up my horoscope.

Does this profile of Libra resemble you in any way?

In some ways it does. I'm definitely a big romantic and I'd do anything to avoid a row. I like working in a group and I am a bit of a ditherer when it comes to making up my mind. Yes, I can be lazy and I definitely like all the best things in life, but doesn't everyone? But I'm definitely not smarmy! Write that down!

Do you believe in star signs and horoscopes?

I think it's all a bit of a laugh. I wouldn't plan my day around what my horoscope said, and I wouldn't avoid people because they are the wrong star sign!"